Rotkäppchen
Märchen-Malbuch

Little Red Riding Hood
Fairy Tale and Coloring Pages

Bilingual Book in German and English
by Charles Perrault and Svetlana Bagdasaryan.
Translated into German by Moritz Hartmann

Es war einmal in einem Dorf ein kleines Mädchen, das hübscheste, das man sich vorstellen konnte; seine Mutter war ganz in das Kind vernarrt, und noch vernarrter war seine Grossmutter. Diese gute Frau liess ihm ein rotes Käppchen machen, und weil ihm das so gut stand, nannte man es überall nur Rotkäppchen.

Eines Tages sprach seine Mutter, die gerade Fladen gebacken und zubereitet hatte, zu ihm: "Sieh einmal nach, wie es deiner Grossmutter geht, denn man hat mir gesagt, sie sei krank. Bring ihr einen Fladen und diesen kleinen Topf Butter."

Rotkäppchen lief sogleich davon, um zu seiner Grossmutter zu gehen, die in einem anderen Dorf wohnte.

* * *

Once upon a time there lived in a village a little country girl, the prettiest creature that had ever been seen. Her mother was very fond of her, and her grandmother loved her still more. This good woman made for her a little red riding hood, which fit her so well that everybody called her Little Red Riding Hood.

One day her mother, having made some pies, said to her, "Go, my dear, and see how your grandmother does, for I hear she has been very ill; bring her the pies and this little pot of butter."

Little Red Riding Hood set out immediately to go to her grandmother's, who lived in another village.

Als es durch einen Wald kam, traf es den Gevatter Wolf, der grosse Lust hatte, es zu fressen; aber er wagte es nicht wegen einiger Holzfäller, die in dem Wald waren. Er fragte es, wohin es gehe. Das arme Mädchen, das nicht wusste, dass es gefährlich war, stehenzubleiben und einem Wolf zuzuhören, sagte zu ihm: "Ich besuche meine Grossmutter und bringe ihr einen Fladen und einen kleinen Topf Butter, die ihr meine Mutter schickt."

"Wohnt sie denn sehr weit?" fragte der Wolf.

"Oh ja", sagte das kleine Rotkäppchen, "es ist noch ein Stück hinter der Mühle, die Ihr da unten seht, im ersten Haus vom Dorf."

"Na schön!" sagte der Wolf. "Dann will ich sie auch besuchen. Ich gehe diesen Weg hier, und du gehst den anderen Weg damal sehen, wer eher da ist."

* * *

As she was going through the woods, she met the gaffer wolf, who wanted to eat her up; but he dared not, because of the loggers working near in the forest. He asked her where she was going. The poor child, who did not know that it was dangerous to stop and talk to a wolf, said to him, "I am going to see my grandmother, and bring her the pies and little pot of butter that my mother sent."

"Does she live far?" asked the wolf.

"Oh, yes," answered Little Red Riding Hood; "it is behind that mill you see there; the first house you come to in the village."

"Well," said the wolf, "and I'll go and see her, too. I'll go this way, and you go that way, and we shall see who will get there first."

Der Wolf lief aus Leibeskräften den Weg, der kürzer war, und das kleine Mädchen ging den längeren Weg, wobei es seine Freude daran hatte, Haselnüsse zu sammeln, Schmetterlingen nachzujagen und Sträusse aus den Blümchen zu binden, die es fand. Der Wolf brauchte nicht lange, um zum Haus der Grossmutter zu gelangen. Er klopfte an: poch, poch.

"Wer ist da?"

"Ich bin Euer Töchterchen Rotkäppchen", sagte der Wolf, indem er seine Stimme verstellte, "und bringe Euch einen Fladen und einen kleinen Topf Butter, die Euch meine Mutter schickt."

Die gute Grossmutter, die im Bett lag, weil sie ein wenig krank war, rief ihm zu: "Zieh den Pflock, dann fällt der Riegel."

* * *

The wolf began to run as fast as he could, taking the shortest way, and the little girl went by the longest way, amusing herself by gathering nuts, running after butterflies, and picking flowers. Not before long wolf reached the old woman's house. He knocked at the door — knock, knock, knock.

"Who's there?" called the grandmother.

"It is your granddaughter, Little Red Riding Hood," replied the wolf, imitating the girl's voice. "Mother sent you some pies and a little pot of butter."

The good grandmother, who was in bed, because she was somewhat ill, cried out, "Pull the bobbin, and the latch will go up."

Der Wolf zog den Pflock, und die Tür ging auf. Er stürzte sich auf die gute Frau und verschlang sie im Nu, denn er hatte schon seit über drei Tagen nichts gegessen. Darauf schloss er die Tür wieder und ging hin und legte sich in das Bett der Grossmutter, um dort auf das kleine Rotkäppchen zu warten, das einige Zeit später kam und an die Tür klopfte: poch, poch.

"Wer ist da?"

Als Rotkäppchen die rauhe Stimme des Wolfs hörte, hatte es erst Angst, aber weil es meinte, die Grossmutter sei erkältet, gab es zur Antwort: "Ich bin Euer Töchterchen Rotkäppchen und bringe Euch einen Fladen und einen kleinen Topf Butter, die Euch meine Mutter schickt."

* * *

The wolf pulled the bobbin, and the door opened. He fell upon the old woman and swallowed her, for he had not eaten anything for more than three days. He then shut the door, went into the grandmother's bed, and waited for Little Red Riding Hood, who came sometime afterward and knocked at the door — knock, knock, knock.

"Who's there?" called the wolf.

Little Red Riding Hood, hearing the hoarse voice of the wolf, was at first afraid; but thinking her grandmother had a cold, answered, "This is your granddaughter, Little Red Riding Hood. Mother sent you some pies and a little pot of butter."

Der Wolf rief ihm zu, indem er seine Stimme ein wenig sanfter machte: "Zieh den Pflock, dann fällt der Riegel."

Rotkäppchen zog den Pflock, und die Tür ging auf.

Als der Wolf sah, dass es hereinkam, versteckte er sich im Bett unter der Decke und sagte zu ihm: "Stell den Fladen und den kleinen Topf Butter auf den Backtrog und leg dich zu mir."

Das kleine Rotkäppchen geht hin und legt sich in das Bett, wo es zu seinem allergrössten Erstaunen sah, wie seine Grossmutter ohne Kleider beschaffen war.

* * *

The wolf cried out to her, softening his voice a little, "Pull the bobbin, and the latch will go up."

Little Red Riding Hood pulled the bobbin, and the door opened.

The wolf, seeing her come in, said to her, hiding himself under the bedclothes, "Put the pies and little pot of butter somewhere, and come and lie down with me."

Little Red Riding Hood went into bed, where she was much surprised to see how her grandmother looked in her night-clothes.

Es sagte zu ihr:
"Grossmutter, was habt Ihr für grosse Arme!"
"Damit ich dich besser umfangen kann, mein Kind!"
"Grossmutter, was habt Ihr für grosse Beine!"
"Damit ich besser laufen kann, mein Kind!"
"Grossmutter, was habt Ihr für grosse Ohren!"
"Damit ich besser hören kann, mein Kind!"
"Grossmutter, was habt Ihr für grosse Augen!"
"Damit ich besser sehen kann, mein Kind!"
"Grossmutter, was habt Ihr für grosse Zähne!"
"Damit ich dich fressen kann!"
Und mit diesen Worten stürzte sich der böse Wolf auf Rotkäppchen und frass es.

* * *

She said to her, "Grandmamma, what big arms you have!"
"All the better to hug you with, my dear."
"Grandmamma, what great legs you have!"
"All the better to run with, my child."
"Grandmamma, what great ears you have!"
"All the better to hear with, my child."
"Grandmamma, what great eyes you have!"
"All the better to see with, my child."
"Grandmamma, what great teeth you have!"
"All the better to eat you up with."
And, saying these words, this wicked wolf fell upon Little Red Riding Hood, and ate her all up.

In diesem Moment kam der Jäger aus dem Wald vorbei. Er sah ein Haus und beschloss zu bleiben, um nach einem Glas Wasser zu fragen. Der Jäger war auf der Suche nach einem großen Wolf, der das Dorf in Angst und Schrecken versetzt hat.

Der Jäger hörte ein seltsames Geräusch aus dem Hause, er schaute durchs Fenster, und sah wie der Wolf im Bett der Oma lag und schnarchte. "Der Wolf! Er wird mir dieses mal nicht entkommen!" rief der Jäger.

Er öffnete den Bauch des Wolfes, aus diesem zu seiner Überraschung wohlbehalten die Großmutter und das Rotkäppchen auftauchte.

* * *

At this moment a hunter emerged from the forest. He saw the house and decided to stop and ask for a glass of water. He was looking for a big wolf who had been terrorizing the village.

The hunter heard a strange whistling inside the house. He looked through the window and saw the big wolf snoring on Grandma's bed. "The wolf! He won't escape me this time!" cried the hunter.

The hunter opened the wolf's stomach, and, to his surprise, out popped the unharmed Grandma and Little Red Riding Hood.

ACKNOWLEDGEMENT

Special thanks to Heiko Falkenstein and Olga Hofmann for their help with translation and editing.

Printed in Germany
by Amazon Distribution
GmbH, Leipzig